Etienne Felix Berlioux

The Slavetrade in Africa in 1872

Etienne Felix Berlioux

The Slavetrade in Africa in 1872

ISBN/EAN: 9783743419056

Manufactured in Europe, USA, Canada, Australia, Japa

Cover: Foto ©ninafisch / pixelio.de

Manufactured and distributed by brebook publishing software
(www.brebook.com)

Etienne Felix Berlioux

The Slavetrade in Africa in 1872

THE
SLAVE TRADE IN AFRICA
IN
1872.

PRINCIPALLY CARRIED ON FOR THE SUPPLY OF TURKEY, EGYPT, PERSIA, AND ZANZIBAR.

BY

ETIENNE FELIX BERLIOUX,

PROFESSOR OF HISTORY IN THE LYCEUM OF LYONS.

From the French.

WITH A PREFACE

BY

JOSEPH COOPER.

LONDON:

EDWARD MARSH, 12, BISHOPSGATE STREET WITHOUT.

MDCCCLXXII.

PREFACE.

MANY persons suppose the Slave-trade to be a thing of the past—something truly horrible in former times, but an evil which happily now no longer exists.

To such, as well as to those who are only partially acquainted with the subject, it will be startling to learn that parts of the great Continent of Africa equal in extent to the whole of Europe, are at this moment devastated by the Slave-trade, and that hundreds of thousands of victims fall a prey to it every year.

We may well be thankful that the Slave-trade, carried on by professedly Christian people, from Western Africa to the Atlantic coasts for more than three hundred years, has at length disappeared.

As to the existing Slave-trade, which is carried on principally from Northern and Central Africa eastwards, the writer of the following work has been at special pains to collect from all authentic sources the most recent information on the subject.

M. Berlioux, its author, the able Professor of History in the Lyceum of Lyons, published a more extensive volume* on the subject early in the year 1870, to which the reader is referred for further information, especially so far as the subject is affected by the various religious creeds of the people engaged in it.

It is scarcely necessary to say, that M. Berlioux's great object in devoting his time and talents to the work, is the abolition of the Slave-trade. He remarks with much truth, that the first step towards the abolition of an evil, is its exposure to the public eye.

In sympathy with this view, I respectfully and earnestly solicit for his work the careful perusal of all those who feel any interest in the progress of civilisation, and the welfare of their fellow-men.

---

* "La Traite Orientale, Histoire des chasses à l'homme organisées en Afrique depuis quinze ans, pour les marchés de l'Orient," par Etienne Félix Berlioux, Professeur d'Histoire au Lycée Impérial de Lyons, avec une carte des pays parcourus par les traitants.—Paris: Librairie de Guillemin et Cie., rue Richelieu, 14.

Looking at the fact that so many years have been spent in abolishing the Western Slave-trade, it cannot be matter of surprise, considering the comparatively little public attention that has been attracted to it, that no progress has yet been made towards its extinction in the East.

As M. Berlioux has truly remarked, whenever the Powers of Europe shall agree to bring their united moral influence to bear upon it, the Slave-trade will cease to exist.

But were this the case to-day, it might at any moment be revived, unless some change is wrought in the mind of the Mussulmans of Egypt and Turkey on the subject of slavery itself.

So long as slavery exists as an institution, there will be markets for slaves, and a temptation to revive the Slave-trade.

If this be true, it is of the last importance that with the influence of the European Powers to put down the Slave-trade, a simultaneous effort should be made to promote enlightened views on the subject among the people of Turkey, Egypt, and Persia.

Much has been said of the impediment which the religious belief of the Mussulman offers to the abolition, both of the Slave-trade and slavery. Are there not grounds to believe that this difficulty is somewhat exaggerated ? Whether we look at Turkey, Egypt, or Persia, we may see some reason to believe that this is the case.

With regard to Turkey, the Sultan in a firman on the Circassian Slave-trade in 1854, so far from offering any defence of slavery on the ground of the Ottoman Faith, uses these remarkable words on the religious bearing of the question— "Man is the most noble of all the creatures God has formed, in making him free ; selling people as animals, or articles of furniture, is contrary to the will of the Sovereign Creator."

Then, with regard to Egypt, in the interview which the deputation from the Paris Conference had with the Viceroy and his Minister, Nubar Pacha, in 1867, this subject was specially noticed. His Highness reminded the deputation of the fact, that Africa had been desolated by Christian nations for ages, although slavery was condemned by the Christian religion. He said that the religion of the Mussulman did not forbid slavery, but " it was a horrible institution, inconsistent with civilisation and humanity, and that therefore it must be abolished." He further remarked "that the civilisation and progress of Egypt depended upon its abolition; and were the Slave-trade stopped, slavery would disappear in fifteen years, or very few traces of it would remain, because it would not be recruited from without."

As to Persia, in the year 1846 a correspondence took place between the British Government and Persia, relative to the abolition of the African Slave-trade.

In consequence of the opposition of the Shah to its abolition on religious grounds, Colonel Shiel procured from six priests of reputation in Tehran their opinions upon the subject. The following is the reply of one of them; the other answers were substantially the same :—"Decree.— Selling male and female slaves is an abomination according to the noble faith. 'The worst of men is the seller of men,' (tradition of Mohammed). God it is who knows." Sealed by Moollah Meerza Mahmood Andermanee.

Thus, whether we look at Turkey, Egypt, or Persia, whatever sanction the Koran may afford to slavery and the Slave-trade, some homage at least is paid to better principles.

There can be no doubt but that Europeans of several nations are still secretly engaged more or less directly in the Slave-trade.

James Richardson, the estimable African traveller, who fell a victim to his exertions near Kouka, in Bornou, in the year 1851, arrived at the conclusion that much of the Eastern Slave-trade he witnessed in Northern and Eastern Africa, had its origin with European merchants, under French and English protection. Consuls and Consular agents are in some cases engaged in trade on their own accounts, and though there are among them upright and high-minded men, as a general rule they do not represent the good intentions of the Governments whose appointments they hold.

It is absolutely necessary, if any real progress is to be made in the right direction, that honest consuls should be appointed, and in order to secure such, they must be properly paid for the service.

Probably there are few who have paid attention to the effect of slavery in Eastern countries, who do not see that its existence has much to do in producing the lethargy and sensuality which are so destructive to all the best interests of the people.

It forms a sort of enclosure, within which the Mussulman lives a peculiar life—" an outwork behind which he finds a refuge from the influence of civilisation and Christianity.

" Destroy it, and his existence will undergo a change, and he will become a different person altogether."

One of the greatest bars to the civilisation of the East is to be found in the conduct of professing Christians, which instead of commending their faith to the followers of Mohammed, has been in many instances such as to cause the name of Christ to be blasphemed. With too much truth it has been stated, that " never in the course of their history have Mohammedans been brought into contact with any form of Christianity that was not too degenerate in its rites, its doctrines, and its effects, to be worthy of their esteem."*

Happily there are not wanting, on the part of professedly Christian nations, some indications of

---

* For information as to the conduct of professing Christians among the people of Eastern nations, the reader will do well to refer to the highly important work of the Hon. Henry Stanley, entitled " East and West." Hatchard and Co., 1865.

a disposition to pursue a wiser and juster course of conduct towards the less enlightened portion of the human race.

May we not therefore hope that this stumbling-block to the progress of civilisation, and to the reception of the Gospel, may be removed, and that the nations of Europe will combine in one great moral effort for the entire abolition of slavery and the Slave-trade. However great and apparently insurmountable the obstacles may be, the great work will assuredly be accomplished.

May it please the Almighty Father of all, to hasten the blessed change in benighted Africa, and so to prepare the way for the coming of that day when from the rising of the sun to the going down of the same, the name of the Lord shall be great among the Gentiles, and in every place incense shall be offered unto His name, and a pure offering.

JOSEPH COOPER.

Essex Hall, Walthamstow,
  First Month, 1872.

THE SLAVE TRADE IN AFRICA IN 1872.

INTRODUCTION.

THERE is a work, one of the glories of our age, in which Humanity must rejoice, and of which England, in particular, may be proud; it is the Abolition of Slavery in the colonies of Christian peoples. In them, the negro has ceased to be game which is hunted—an article of merchandise to be sold—a beast of burden goaded to labour by the lash.

On December 31st, 1868, the Mixed Commission Court established at the Cape of Good Hope by the Governments of Great Britain, the United States, and Portugal, declared that it had not been called upon to judge one single case of slave-trade during the year then closing.

In consequence of this, Lord Clarendon announced that these three nations had concluded to discontinue the Commission. There could be no longer any reason for its continuance, as the slave-trade was abolished on the western coasts of Africa.

Thus it may be said that the western traffic is dead,

but the friends of humanity must not too speedily rejoice, for whilst the evil has disappeared on one side, it has manifested itself on the other—as widespread, as distressing and as hideous as ever.

This latter trade, made known only within the last few years to civilised nations, and still little known to the public in general, is so dreadful that we should be tempted to disbelieve the accounts, were they not attested by the most indubitable evidence.

This great man-hunt, of which we once knew nothing, carries off annually 70,000 prisoners—the number of the dead that it leaves behind is incalculable; the total certainly cannot be less than 350,000, but it probably amounts to 550,000. The countries in which it exists and to which it introduces incendiarism, devastation and murder, are of much greater extent than the whole of Europe.

Let not these figures be deemed exaggerations, neither let these horrors be denied, because they have remained so long unknown. To prove the number of victims, the depositions of witnesses have been examined and compared; but as the witnesses themselves have not seen all, the reality must be still more terrible than the picture they have drawn.

If these facts have been concealed up to the present time, it is because the guilty parties have taken the greatest care to hide them; the crime has been committed in countries unfrequented by our travellers, which is another cause of our ignorance. The culpable parties have also been much on their guard, because many of them, belonging to western nations, have been unwilling that the vile source whence they obtained their riches should be revealed.

This new slave-trade is carried on for the eastern markets and from the eastern coasts of Africa. The slave hunts are organised in three regions,—in the interior of the African continent, on the borders of the Upper Nile, and on the coasts of the Indian Ocean.

The countries where the slaves are sold are Egypt, Arabia, and all those in possession of Mussulmans. It has taken many years of effort to destroy the western slave-trade, which diplomacy has not lost sight of since the year 1815. At length success is achieved, and not only has the western slave-trade been abolished, but slavery itself has disappeared almost everywhere.

Following the example of other great nations, Portugal has almost abolished it, and though Spain and Brazil still retain slavery, they are taking some steps towards its abolition and will not much longer maintain an institution condemned by the whole civilised world.

In the East, a long time will be required to bring about a reform, and it will prove very difficult, if slavery itself be the question; for there, the manners, traditions, and religious creeds, all encourage and protect it.

A great and complete moral renovation will be necessary to effect its disappearance. But to destroy the transport and importation of negroes as slaves, Europe has but seriously to insist upon it.

The vessels in which the prisoners of the man-hunters are crowded, file off, so to speak, before our colonies and pass through the midst of our fleets. They belong to peoples incapable of resisting the orders of Europe, because the uncivilised men who command them can rely neither on their strength, nor on their ability to escape the pursuit of the cruisers.

Our ignorance, and the negligence of our Governments, alone have permitted this disgraceful traffic to continue to this day. It will cease when we have become better informed, and are possessed of more zeal.

The error of Europe, in this respect, is one of the strangest and the most difficult to explain; but the part taken by England, in one respect, is still more extra-ordinary. This Power, which was so zealous against the Western slave trade, made a terrible mistake when she sanctioned it in the East. Although this error is about to be abandoned, we may still speak of it, and indeed must do so, in order to hasten the reform.

That which England would have indignantly refused to

the United States and to Spain, she formally granted to the Sultan of Zanzibar; which concession has had the most disastrous results.

When England shall have annulled these treaties, the civilised nations will soon be able to unite in destroying the Eastern slave-trade. Already the work of reparation has commenced. The Committee appointed by the English Parliament to examine the treaties with Zanzibar, have just demanded their repeal.

Without entering on all the conclusions of the Report, or approving all the articles, we must applaud the decision of the members of this Committee, when they agree in urging the entire abandonment of the slave-trade. The public will undoubtedly encourage this work of reform, and demand the total and immediate abolition of the Eastern slave-trade as soon as it becomes acquainted with the subject.

To expose the horrors of the slave-trade everywhere, as they at present exist, is the object of this little work.

CHAPTER I.

In the first step we take in the examination of this great subject, we find in the train of the man-hunters horrors which were unknown to the former slave-trade.

When the negro was brought to the coasts of Guinea, to be sold to the American purchasers, he had not to make long days' marches across the dreadful solitudes of Sahara. In the new traffic, organised for the markets of the East, the black that has just been severed from his family and deprived of his liberty, while suffering unheard-of cruelties, must traverse the vast plains of sand, which separate the interior of Africa from the borders of the Mediterranean, in order to arrive at the place of his future servile existence.

The desert with its scorching sands, devoid of verdure and springs, with its storm-driven dust that buries caravans, seems more terrible than the Ocean, and to cross it requires a more lengthened period.

From the town of Tripoli to the Lake Tchad, there are nearly twenty degrees, an extent of land more than twice

and a-half the length of Great Britain. It is by this
route that the convoys of negroes are driven, by their
pitiless masters, condemned, under the burning sun, to
the tortures of thirst, hunger and fatigue. It is a long
funereal march in the midst of the solitude of the
desert.

From time to time one of the miserable company falls,
to rise no more; his fellow-prisoners make no halt to
cover his body even with a little sand. Let it not be
supposed that this is a picture of the imagination only.
Monsieur Rohfs, who was an eye-witness of these things
during his explorings between the years 1865 and 1867,
and who was the first to denounce these mysteries of
crime, gives them to us in frightful detail:—

"On both sides of the road," he says, "we see the
blanched bones of the victimised slaves—skeletons still
covered by the katoun, the clothing of the blacks. The
traveller who knows nothing of the road to Bournou, has
only to follow these scattered remains and he will not be
misguided."

The merchants take a singular precaution, lest the slave
should rob them of a few drops of water: they place the
leathern bottle in such a position, that the orifice is turned
towards the head of the camel that carries it. The
animal, which is itself athirst, begins to cry as soon as the
precious vessel is touched, and thus the attempt to par-

take of its contents would be discovered. Thus thirst, as
well as bodily fatigue, has innumerable victims.

When evening draws on, the miserable groups often
have not physical strength to drag their wearied bodies to
the springs that might slake their parched mouths.

Sometimes the wind causes the mouths of the wells to
be filled with sand. When this is the case, some of the
negroes, not having sufficient strength to wait until the
needed clearance is made, die; and their companions have
barely the strength to remove the corpses.

The traveller whose name we have before mentioned,
relates that he met with a certain spring surrounded with
what might emphatically be called a field of the dead:
there, bones were laid about in heaps. His servants,
who had drawn water from this spring, without observing
it carried off in the bucket the skull of a man. These
human skeletons, mingled as they are with the bones
of the lower animals, are the remains of slaves.

On leaving these frightful solitudes where man is
proved to be more merciless than the desert, reaching the
zone of the forests, the eye is rejoiced at the sight of rich
vegetation, flowers and lakes, these latter giving to the
soil an endless source of fertility.

But in the midst of Nature which God has made so
rich, sorrowful reflections come over the mind. This
privileged land is the theatre of slavery and the home of

the man-hunter. The large city of Kouka, in the vicinity of Lake Tchad, the capital of Bournou, is one of the greatest marts for this human merchandise.

On the Square, the best adapted for the slave-markets, one is sure every day to find several hundreds; but on Monday, the great sale day, they may be numbered by thousands: the blacks are there exhibited in their pitiable plight, partially covered with miserable tatters. The wholesale merchants and connoisseurs have no need to be attracted by a more delicate exposition, such as that which one would meet with in a retail purchase.

The slave is examined with care, taking measure of his height, opening his mouth, counting his teeth, asking questions about his appetite, &c., &c. The price demanded is according to the age, strength and colour of the prisoner, and varies from half a sovereign to five pounds for the current merchandise. Is this all that a man is worth, and is this the estimate put on human liberty? There are other markets at which the slave is considered of still less value.

But whence come all these wretched beings? It is here that the Eastern traffic is presented to us under a particular aspect, such as it did not assume on the Western coasts of Africa in the organised commerce of slaves. Man-hunting, which supplies the victims for these markets, is not only encouraged by the brutal ferocity of the chief of a tribe; it is considered an act commanded by religion.

The Sultan, who goes to make razzias at the head of warriors, with whom he divides the booty, by an impious aberration believes that he performs a pious work in spreading devastation around him. This is the effect of the old Mahomedan influence, and the sword of the knights follows the infidel enemies of the Koran.

The accusation is a solemn one. "The Sultan," M. Rohlf informs us, "is a wholesale merchant himself. What is that in which he deals? What is it? why his brother man; he procures such for his own benefit by razzias over the surrounding peoples, or over his own subjects, so long as these latter have not embraced Islamism." In order to understand the abominations connected with the Eastern slave-trade, we must rid ourselves of our European ideas, and enter a new world, in which men and events have in store for us more than one subject of surprise.

It is easy to form an opinion as to the importance of this slave-traffic in this region, when we know the extent of the caravans that convey the negroes from Kouka. During many weeks, the preparations and the departure fill the capital with noise and bustle. Long files of camels are laden with provisions, two thousand armed men serve as an escort, and the human flock altogether counts four thousand heads. For the Sultan, for his horsemen, for his wholesale merchants, for the entire city, the caravan season is a great annual festivity; for the slave, it is the moment of banishment, the renewal of sufferings, and perhaps the eve of his death. Very speedily all this multitude has taken a northern direction, and soon it disappears from the side of the desert.

But this crowd of unhappy beings, these miserable creatures of all ages—children, young men, old men and women—where are they going? What agricultural or industrial labour demands them from the Eastern coast? What route will they take, since the north of Africa, the borders of the Mediterranean, belong to those Powers which proscribe the traffic? It is on account of these apparent difficulties, and because of the mysteries in which the Oriental trade has been involved, that it has been able to conceal itself, until the present day, from the observation of Europe.

We refrain, for the moment, from replying to the first of these enquiries. We shall learn later what becomes of these unfortunates.

We are about to see how these flocks of men, in spite of their number, can, without hindrance or denouncement, cross those countries in which the slave-trade is prohibited.

Between Tripoli and Kouka lies the Oasis of the Fezzan,

in which the Porte holds a garrison of five hundred men, commanded by a Kobrassi.

In 1865, the period when M. Rohlfs crossed the Fezzan, many things were related to him respecting the local administration. He was witness at that time of the following scene:—On a certain day, the Doctor of the garrison presented himself at the residence of M. Rohlfs, begging him to dismiss his servant, and to close the door; he then entered upon the subject of the slave-trade, and, according to his statement, there was an understanding between the authorities and the slave-traders. These latter only guide their convoys by night. As soon as the caravan arrives, the corporal of the watch begins to count heads: the Kobrassi presides at the opening of the city gates, and the Kaimakan receives a report; he, as Governor, demands this, because his perquisite is the sum of two mahbouds (ten francs, or about eight shillings English money,) per slave; this is regarded as a small gratuity for his son-in-law, Kaivasbacha. This contraband proceeding must be very profitable, if we are to believe the good Doctor. The Kaimakan had allowed at least four thousand slaves to pass through the city of Moursouk, in 1865, but the number might have amounted to ten thousand who crossed the Oasis. This information was of the greatest importance; but it is sad to be obliged to say, that in giving it, the Doctor acted not from a feeling of humanity, but merely from jealousy: in this work of lucrative deception, the Kaimakan had not given a single mahboud either to the Kobrassi or to the Doctor.

This, then, is the manner in which the slave-trade is continued in defiance of all laws. Though the law condemn it, public opinion sees in it only a national institution which it is not forced to give up; the authorities shut their eyes, or favour a commerce that assures to them handsome revenues.

As for the supervision of European Powers, it has been as nothing for many years past. The Consuls confine themselves to the principal ports on the coast, where the traffickers never come; the consular agents, in the interior, are not always wisely chosen, so that their surveillance is not efficient—both parties frequently fail with respect to the knowledge necessary to render it so.

It seems established by evidence that the traffic in slaves, far from decreasing, is more flourishing than ever. An old inhabitant of Kouka declares, that during the last twenty years, a greater number had been sent from Bournou, than had been, previously, for one hundred years.

The merchants, whom the police of Europe disturbed in some places, no doubt concluded that their traffic would be less interfered with beyond the solitudes of Sahara.

CHAPTER II.

THE MIDDLE VALLEY OF THE NILE.

THE revelations which we receive from the borders of the Nile are still more strange, more sorrowful.

Two circumstances add a mournful interest to the spectacle which the slave-trade presents to us in this its second stage. Here the man-hunters are no longer savages in whose uncivilised condition may be pleaded some extenuation of their crimes. Many among them are Europeans belonging to nations the most refined.

These men, the more learned, therefore the more to be dreaded, come with resources with which civilisation has furnished them, to preside over a moral devastation.

We shall see more of this devastation somewhat later. In the desert, we have seen the victims dying with fatigue, the skeletons of those to whom the agony of thirst with the burning sands had proved fatal; but our information is not yet complete. We have not been present at the hunt itself; we have not seen the hunters at work; we have not heard the sound of the musketry, the cries of the fugitives: we have not beheld villages on fire, the dying writhing in agony, and the more infuriated prisoners fastened by their first galling fetters.

We may well wonder that these horrors of the Oriental slave-trade have been so long hidden from the view of Christian nations, but we find in the revelations which now reach us from all quarters, at one and the same time, an extraordinary coincidence.

At the moment in which M. Rhôlfs informs us of the traffic of Sahara, man-hunting is made known to us by several other travellers—Messrs. Baker, Speke, Henglin, Lejean, and the Mesdames Tinné. In their united testimony we have much important information.

The Egyptian city of Khartoun, situated at the junction of the two Niles, almost at the same distance from Alexandria as is Kouka from the east of Tripoli, is the grand centre of this iniquitous commerce and the residence of the contractors. It is there that the large societies of the traffickers are organised. There they find bankers who lend them money at an interest as high as cent. per cent.; the dockyards of the city prepare for them fleets of vessels to re-ascend the valley of the Nile; the neighbouring populations, accustomed to live by plunder, furnish them with horsemen and foot soldiers; some master scoundrel is placed at the head of these bands; they collect provisions for a year or more. When all is in readiness, on a fine day, the wind blowing from the

North, the whole expedition suddenly disappears in a southern direction. No one can tell what is about to be done. Should any more inquisitive traveller wish to know what will become of these men, let him beware. They would begin by alarming him as to the difficulties of the voyage—the morasses, fevers, ferocious animals, and negroes still more terrible. If he persist in his enquiries, they give him to understand that there is connected with these solitudes some frightful mystery which he must not know, and that death awaits the individual who is bold enough to despise counsel. They say in explanation of the expedition that the armed men are appointed to hunt elephants, and to protect the enterprise against the attacks of the merchant trader. These latter, not contented with the exchange of their small articles of merchandise for ivory, desire to obtain the monopoly of so lucrative a commerce for themselves. Indeed every year large cargoes of ivory are sent to Khartoun. Slaves have not appeared there since Turkey prohibited the importation of the negroes fifteen years ago. Secret correspondents come to conduct them beyond the city by the desert to their destination, of which of course they know nothing. It is by these means that the enormities of the slave trade have been concealed, as with an impenetrable veil.

The following circumstance, however, furnishes some important information on the subject:—

The death of a Frenchman was one day announced, who had been at the head of a considerable establishment, and was everywhere known as a merchant in horses, and in elephants' teeth; he wished in life to be regarded as a gentleman.

He had, by dint of labour, reached the high position of his ancestors; but what did his books, which had been kept with scrupulous exactness, disclose?

He had traded, not only in ivory and horses, but in slaves. The supplies, the mysterious correspondence, the number of livery servants, all were there indicated with a precision very unfortunate for the reputation of the deceased. The truth began to appear, and the operations and proceedings of the would-be gentleman were made known.

He, no doubt, did business in ivory; but by a method as economical as dishonest, he procured this article of merchandize. His soldiers carried off by turns, provisions elephants' teeth, oxen, and slaves; in fact, all that fell into their hands. The oxen not only furnished food for the troop, but were used also as money with which they paid for ivory to the surrounding tribes. Oxen are riches; perhaps the most esteemed by uncivilised populations.

The negroes have a similar destiny, and are sometimes given in payment to the very traffickers who had been employed in carrying them off.

The French merchant employed an Arab smuggler and horse jockey to exchange slaves for horses, but nevertheless, with a bold front, professed to be at the head of a house as honest in its character, as it was flourishing in its condition. He assumed the refined manners of a gentleman; but in these expeditions, he signalised himself as a finished barbarian; nevertheless it is probable that there is put to his account a portion of the glory of his rivals. History, which loves to simplify statements, sometimes heaps upon certain heroes all the exploits of an entire generation. However, through this *exposé*, increased light has come to the world, relative to the iniquity of the slave traffic; and it has ended by our having a clear view of the mysteries concealed, with such great care, for so lengthened a period.

Although a single traveller might be arrested on his way, it would be difficult indeed to stop the progress of a large expedition like that of Mesdames Tinné, or to overcome an obstinate decision like that of Mr. Baker. With them we shall enter this land of evil omens, that has been witness to so many crimes, but which will, we hope, soon see both liberty and civilisation.

At the present time, caution is absolutely necessary. The vessels which cross each other on the river, carrying all the banners of the universe, are raised aloft by wicked pirates. One day, when Mesdames Tinné's captain wished to accost one of these boats, it was intimated to him, by the firing of a gun, that he had better retire.

Some judgment may be formed of the dreadful devastations which ravage the borders of the White Nile, by the account of that which took place in 1864.

According to several sources of information, a large fleet, counting sixty vessels, brought its numberless equipages to the countries of the Shillouks, and of the Denkas, situated to the south of Khartoun. After the Campaign, they collected together the prisoners destined to slavery. A thousand horsemen were sent out to scour the country, and to bring in, by the aid of the foot soldiery, crowds of captives. The Chief of the Egyptian Police, who perhaps, by way of exception, decided to fulfil his duty, captured twelve vessels, and on these were found seventeen hundred slaves, so that if the other portion of the fleet received as many prisoners, it is evident that one expedition alone is able to carry off eight or nine thousand heads. The number of deaths may be estimated by that of the captives.

Whilst the cavalry and infantry are scouring the country, there remain on the borders of the river only a few encampments, to protect the vessels, and watch the retreat. But, beside these provisional stations, there are permanent ones, where many of the slave dealers live. as little princes, and settle down as sovereigns, with their bandits and their subjects.

It is easy to comprehend the terror which these spread around them. On one occasion, at a village where some of the houses were burning, when Miss Tinné was passing by, the unhappy negroes innocently besought her to declare herself their protectress, and to defend them from the bandits.

These bandits or robbers, who establish themselves along the White Nile, in the country which extends in length to a thousand kilometers to the south of Khartoun, belong almost exclusively to the Arab race. In the interior will be found two other classes of adventurers, Europeans, and half-civilised Orientalists. The Europeans use the greatest precautions; and in order to avoid being discovered, find it necessary to leave immense solitudes behind them.

Leaving them at present, let us observe what takes place in a quarter more especially inhabited by those from the East. The territory that they work is a muddy region, which spreads over a space from the equator to ten degrees north latitude.

This country precedes that mountain range in which the Messrs. Baker and Speke discovered the extensive lakes whence flows the Nile. It is intersected with morasses and rivers, forming an inextricable maze, in which it is most difficult to trace the man-hunter, and to detect him in his iniquitous course.

It appears that the slave trade has been carried on in these countries only about fifteen years.

In 1863, when the expedition of the Mesdames Tinné arrived here, there was, in the centre of these fever-producing bogs, a kind of fœtid residuum, sending forth a canal somewhat considerable. This canal develops itself around an island which is composed of muddy earth.

In this unhealthy and muddy region, whence arise fevers, and where crocodiles dwell, the slave hunters have established one of their most frequented stations. Twenty vessels are always crowded together in this small port of Meschra, waiting the arrival of the convoys from the interior.

Let us now see how these distant expeditions are organised. Like others, they come from Khartoun, whence they have taken their vessels, with their merchandise and men. For the enrolment of these last, it is calculated that from sixty to a hundred and fifty are required for every settlement they establish. Each company must have soldiers, hunters, interpreters, and clerks : as for domestic servants or slaves, no account is given. The men receive a salary varying from fifty to eighty piastres per month, or otherwise a portion of the benefits from the enterprise, a third of the cattle at least. In addition to this, the soldier can do, on his own account, a little business, such as the selling of lances, arrows and other trifling articles, which he gives to his servants to carry. As for his food, it is a most simple affair, and he is authorised to support himself by robbery and pillage.

There are, however, some things which he cannot procure among the natives when the expedition continues for several years, such as clothing, tobacco, brandy and pearls for barter. The master sells the provision to his men, not forgetting to double, or even triple, the price. The sales and the purchases are inscribed on the books of every one enlisted, and he, on his return, has, in many cases, nothing to receive from his master: his profits are derived alone from his robberies and depredations.

Once arrived at the spot chosen for the operations of the campaign, the merchant, general-in-chief, establishes on the borders of the river a central dépôt, where he brings the munitions purchased at Khartoun, and where the columns of the army bring the ivory collected on their rounds. The establishments of the interior are called Séribes; the number of them varies according to the importance of the country, and the power of the chief-ruler. They are intrenched camps, or the prisons of the African feudality. There is nothing, however, in these store-houses to remind one of our ancient châteaux, for they are constructed but for a time, as it is necessary that the station should be changed according to the requisition of commerce. It is a square of eighty-four paces, surrounded with palisades, in the interior of which there are a certain number of conical huts, used often as habitations, or for merchandise and provisions. The impure beings who dwell in these dens know as little of cleanliness as of justice ; the dungheaps around the Séribes send forth filthy odours; vermin abound, and the most disgusting diseases devour the inhabitants.

The contracting merchant does not always reside at the Séribes, but contents himself with an annual visit to the central dépôt, at the close of Autumn, when the North wind is favourable for those who go from Khartoun. In his place, a Vékil gives orders at the Séribes, who is at the same time governor, soldier and principal clerk, and who regulates the expeditions and makes purchases. It is not an uncommon thing for an old slave or an Arnante to watch, and maintain intact the reputation of robbery which his race has made for itself, non-commissioned officers aiding him to direct this little army.

When the Séribes is completed, all the surrounding countries become the property of the sovereign ruler: this is the law of the Nile, acknowledged by the traffickers, every one of whom respects the frontiers of his neighbour—so long as he has no particular interest in intruding upon them.

The inhabitants of the department of a Séribes become subjects or serfs, and pay taxes in provisions, and articles

of copper or iron. They are obliged to convey the provisions and to supply food to the disengaged soldiery.
All that the natives possess of ivory must be sold exclusively to the chief governor.

A fine tooth of ivory will pay for, from one to ten
bracelets of copper.

From time to time, in order to renew the provisions or
accelerate their commerce, there are *ghazua*, and the purchasing circuits are arranged as an expedition. When
there remains nothing more to buy or to take around the
Séribes, the Vékil sends to a distance a detachment, of
which the strength varies from ten to a hundred men.

These last-named take with them some merchandise to
sell; yet their main business is to seize and carry off
slaves or cattle.

The enterprise is more serious when the natives, warned
by the *ghazuas* going before, have taken arms to defend a
considerable depôt of ivory or of large flocks. In such
cases, several Vékils unite their disposable forces and
make an expedition in common.

All these labours and preparations are the same for
every dealer in ivory, whether he be a European or an
uncivilised Orientalist. The merchants of Western nations,
whilst claiming the profit, avoid being at the head of
their men, thus screening themselves and charging their
responsibility upon their Vékils; whilst the Eastern
merchants are less cautious.

From the learned M. de Heuglin, of the expedition of Mesdames Tinné, we receive these details relative to the Séribes. He is better enabled to give them, having seen and inspected them, and having become acquainted with the inhabitants. He ventured among them unaccompanied, in the hope of penetrating into the countries of the interior of Africa, which are devastated by the slave-hunters. He had for a neighbour the Chief of a company named Abou-Mouri.

Seeing how he was treated, European as he was, powerfully supported and recommended, one may judge of the sufferings which the natives endure. On one occasion, being in want of provisions, and not willing to submit to the exactions of the Séribes, he sent five soldiers and twenty negroes to the country of the Niamnians, to make purchases; but Abou-Mouri was the Lord of the place. Just as the factors had commenced buying, the agents of the merchant lord arrived, who carried off the arms and munitions of the first comers, and placed them in the depôt of a brother of Amouri; some of the negroes who endeavoured to escape were arrested, and fired at on the spot, and one died with hunger; the soldiers were confined in irons for five or six days. At length the Chief of the Séribes adjudged to himself five negroes as slaves; the cause of all these crimes was M. de Heuglin's daring to send his men into a district over which Ali-Abou-Amouri was declared Lord, instead of making his purchases of the Séribes.

On another occasion, in spite of the prohibition of the learned German, one of his soldiers bought some elephants' teeth from the blacks of a certain village. The crime was regarded as serious, for one of the most rigid laws interdicts the sale of ivory to any other than to the government which has reserved to itself this monopoly.

The punishment was signal, the culpable village was surrounded, the chief placed in fetters, his wife shot, and fifty children carried off as slaves.

The negroes, however, who suffer all these horrors, do not lose altogether their spirit and courage; but they have no arms, and do not combine, whilst their adversaries know how to unite when the danger is serious. Sometimes the blacks, though under compulsion, lend their aid to the brigands against the neighbouring peoples.

M. de Heuglin was a witness to one of these unequal combats. On the report of the death of Abou-Mouri, the negroes took up arms to rid themselves of their tyrant rulers; but these latter being warned, called to their assistance the surrounding Séribes; the Vékils were immediately en route with their regular forces and their vassals. They fell on the insurgents before these had commenced the attack; and, to revenge the death of some soldiers who had been taken by surprise, the united forces ravaged the States.

On one occasion, the learned traveller was present at
the triumphal return of the victorious army, in the
Séribak of Biselli, a neighbour of Abou-Mouri.

Blows struck upon the trees of a forest close by announced to the women and children that their husbands
and fathers were returning conquerors. The wives
screamed with joy, the children struck the noquaras, the
great drums suspended between two trees; and the fête
continued for several days, with songs and dances, the
neighbours bringing to the warriors goats and beer. The
chiefs of the Séribes took the booty for their portion;
the negroes, for their part, had only a melancholy joy.

There is, indeed, something profoundly sorrowful in
seeing those grown up children lend to the very beings
who steal and sell them, the assistance of their arms, and
without a consciousness of their acts, give themselves up
to careless and senseless hilarity.

On the negro, impression is easily made, and it as
rapidly passes away; sorrow, like joy, leaves no abiding
trace. On a fine summer's evening when the harvest
is over, and the beer is just brewed, one may hear,
from the summit of the hill, the villages resounding with
the noise of the noquara, and see the fires which enlighten the festivity, and this is continued until day.
These miserable beings think not that the morrow may
find them fastened to the wooden forks of the man-
hunter, who comes to drive them into slavery.

These bandits, so terrible against both travellers and natives, so regardless of all moral law, sometimes quarrel among themselves. M. de Heuglin saw one day a sanguinary struggle in the Séribak of the Chief named Biselli. It was brought about through want, for the chase after a time ceases to be productive, in a country long in a state of devastation. At first desertions commenced, and lightened the ranks; the soldiers left with their arms and baggage, to offer their services to a more fortunate master. Just before this, the Bookkeeper of the camp had arrived with slaves, perhaps carried off from a former possessor.

Thus we see the private life of these brigands, among whom treachery, feasting, blood, drunkenness, in disgusting *mélange*, occupy the days in which they are not employed in devastations. The Book-keeper, a man who knew how to calculate, went in the first place to the house of Abou-Mouri, to assure to himself an engagement, and then returned to finish his preparations and take his leave. He passed the night of the 15th December in drinking with the soldiers, who might at one moment be his protector, at another only like himself.

Suddenly on the morrow, while carrying his game-bag and holding his double-barrel gun, he prepared to depart, but found occasion to quarrel with the Vékil, who ordered the soldiery to arrest him: they, however, remained

immovable, whilst the Secretary made his escape. He
fired on Biselli at the moment he passed before him. The
merchant-lord instantly commanded the twelve Fertists,
who composed his private guard, to pursue the Secretary
and to shoot him. Ten gun-shots resounded at once, but
already the fugitive was out of sight among the tall grass
of the prairie. A hunt was organised, two shots again
were heard, and, a quarter of an hour after, the unhappy
man was brought back, pierced with two balls. M. de
Heuglin replaced the bowels and sewed up the wound, but
in a few moments later he expired. Whilst this was going
on, the soldiers declared to Biselli that they would not
remain with him, and, in less than one hour, they were all
gone—with provisions, wives, children and slaves—some
'to Abou-Mouri, others to rejoin the Mesdames Tinné, who
were encamped at some distance thence. As for Biselli,
he regained a far-off Séribes with two Vékils, his body-
guard, and a dozen slaves whom he had put in chains.

CHAPTER III.

If we wish to see one of the most important centres of the slave-trade, we must re-ascend the Nile as far as the base of the mountains, on which are spread the extensive lakes whence the river takes its rise. It is here that Gondokoro is situated, which station is distant from Khartoun by more than a thousand kilometres, and there the navigation of the great river terminates.

Gondokoro is similar to Meschra, but more extensive, being the grand emporium of the men-hunters. During some months, at the time in which the boats that have quitted Khartoun with fresh provisions arrive, every imaginable ensign is displayed. The caravans come from the interior, descend the neighbouring mountains with their long files of bearers of ivory, and this city presents an extraordinary scene of animation, only to become very shortly afterwards again a desert.

Here the men-hunters, having no occasion to conceal themselves as at Khartoun, and free from all honest restraint, reign as true sovereigns. Their encampments swarm with fettered slaves, and the soldiers, forgetting the little discipline that danger at other times imposes on them, pass their days in quarrelling, drinking, and riot. The firing of guns mingle with the screams of the people, and balls sent hap-hazard whiz in the midst of the tumult of drunkenness. This encampment of the slave-trade is a very hell.

The victims of this pest are not only the dead left on the field of battle, and the prisoners who have been sent, chained by the neck, for some distant captivity, but those whom death or slavery has spared are utterly demoralised by the man-hunter.

The blacks of this country were far superior to those of the morass region; they were a people brave and proud by nature, possessing a remnant of conscientiousness that barbarism never entirely stifled; this inspired them with a sort of integrity which was almost a virtue. But since the entrance of the slave-traders, there are scarcely any inhabitants but mendicants, the inebriate, and characters the most depraved. To use the expression of an author, "the men-hunters have demoralised more than they have murdered and robbed."

It is more particularly at Gondokoro that one is sure to meet with Europeans among the slave-traders. Their presence is recognised by the ability with which they carry on the work of devastation, and it is easy to understand

why they use every precaution to conceal it from the
knowledge of Europe.   Thus, many of the travellers who
have proceeded as far as Gondokoro, have alluded to the
surveillance exercised over them, and the threats and con-
spiracies which are intended to alarm them and to decide
their return by way of Egypt.

But curiosity and science give as much boldness as
crime.   There was, in this valley of the Nile, a problem
to be solved which had engaged the mind of the ancients,
which had interested men of all ages, and which our
epoch, impatient in all its desires, could not leave without
solution.   From what mystic sources flow the mighty
river?   Two Englishmen have returned to bring us the
reply, which is fraught with vast importance to science.
Captain Speke found a first or principal reservoir, the
Lake Victoria, and Mr. Baker has visited the second, the
Albert-Nyanza.   With these discoveries the scientific
world must be enriched; they have brought us another
by which humanity should profit: they have exposed the
ravages of this modern slave-trade, and by thus exposing
them they have prepared the way for their proximate
extinction.

The reports of these two travellers are known, but
probably there will be an advantage in dwelling a little
on some of their relations.   With the experience we
have acquired of slavery in the East, we shall perhaps

better understand than they could, certain events at which
they were present.   Speke was not prepared, either by his
travels or by his previous studies, to know anything of the
traffic of the Nile, and was therefore ignorant of its
horrors.   When he hoped to meet with Egyptian soldiers,
or men sent to protect him, he fell without warning into
the midst of a Séribes.

Just imagine the astonishment of a man plunged, as it
were, suddenly into the midst of a troop of robbers,
finding barbarism where he expected to meet with civilisation.   Relying on the generosity of respectable commerce, he was exposed to the perfidy of smugglers—
saluting military men as men of honour, he finds himself
offering his respect to miserable beings in military dis-
guise.   The Arabian slave-trade which he had elsewhere
met with had not prepared him for this almost European
traffic.   The 3rd December, 1862, after an absence of
several years, after numerous perils, long sufferings, but
a bearer of grand geographical discoveries, for he had
just witnessed the Nile flowing from the Lake Victoria-
Nyanza, with a heart replete with joy, he arrives at a
spot opposite an encampment, with an escort reduced to a
dozen men, and salutes with his musketry those whom
he believes to be Europeans.

Two hundred soldiers at the sound of drums, with flags
waving, hasten to meet him.   The banners, however,

display neither the English colours nor those of
Turkey; the commanding officer belongs not to the
Egyptian army. Speke, with a soul full of emotion,
heartily returns the Mahommedan embrace, but a feeling
of disgust makes him refuse the hug of this would-be
officer. In effect, Mahommed is only a Vékil, and the
men whom he commands are a collection of Nubians,
Egyptians, slaves from all nations, enrolled in the name
of a merchant lord of Khartoun, the Maltais Debono.
Around the camp, robberies and exactions are executed
in the name of the Great Government.

Sometimes it will recklessly carry off several villages, and
enter into alliance with some king; at another time it will
demand six hundred porters for the baggage of the
caravans, under pain of confiscation, and the chiefs of the
tribes must obey the orders of the Government. After
ruining the country, destroying the habitations, entering
into combats with detachments badly armed, distributing
the oxen stolen from other parts, the little army with its
ivory and its slaves returns to Gondokoro.

At the same time when his compatriot took the road
which brought him back to Europe, Mr. Baker travelled
towards the south, in the direction of that moun-
tainous range in which are found the large and famous
lakes. The slave-hunters arrived there at the same time
as himself. They had strenuously endeavoured, by their

intrigues and threats, to derange the plans of so dangerous a witness; but they had not succeeded, and that which they dreaded was realised.

Mr. Baker was an eye-witness to their sanguinary proceedings, was present at their works of destruction, and thus has been able to attest to their crimes with certainty. Here the chase after their fellow-men takes another phase. The principals of houses, who wish not to compromise themselves, remain at Gondokoro, or return to Egypt, and the Vékils alone conduct the expedition.

What is the share of the guilt which ought to be placed to the account of these merchants as respects the atrocities committed by their man-hunters? Do they even know all the crimes that are perpetrated through their means? These are questions which we will not for the moment discuss.

At the period in which Mr. Baker visited these countries, there were three grand chiefs at Godokoro, Chenouda, Kourschid and Debono. It will not be long before the troop of the first-named chief will be exterminated by the natives. As for the detachments of the other two, a considerable time must yet elapse ere they will cease to be the terror of these countries. Mr. Baker, in order to pursue his course, signed a kind of treaty with Kourschid, and had to resign himself to the humilia-

ting alliance. The troop of Debono marched into the
neighbourhood, fighting the negroes, watching the rival
army, negotiating with the chiefs of the country, and
collecting ivory and slaves. These troops of banditti
assume to themselves the air of regular armies; the
Vékils speak of their governments, declare war, sign
treaties, and their operations become military campaigns.
The soldiers of Debono especially distinguished themselves by their insolent audacity, and were sworn
enemies of the reigning prince, but protectors of certain
pretenders. The poor king of the Ounyoro would have
fallen a victim had it not been for the presence of Mr.
Baker, who kindly rescued him. Notwithstanding the
influence of Mr. Baker, these adventurers abandoned themselves at times to their savage instincts.

One day, a Chief of the Court of Kamrasi was by an
order of the king, and with the consent of the Turks,
put to death, because he had sold his ivory to the troop
of Debono, instead of bringing it to the soldiers of
Kourschid. Another time, a father who came to reclaim
his daughter carried off in a razzia, and to offer a ransom
for her, found his child in chains at the entrance of
the Séribak; Ibrahim was absent, and the soldiers, to
rid themselves of the entreaties of this unhappy man,
murdered him. Every feeling of humanity is extinguished
in the heart of these banditti of the Nile, who are even

known at times to applaud an energetic and conquering chief when he inflicts on them a brilliant defeat.

The number of prisoners collected every year by these detachments, who scour the country in the valley of the Nile, it is impossible to calculate; it may, however, be conjectured that the amount rises to about thirty thousand.

The human-hunt is most profitable, and when it is terminated, the Séribaks with their troops go to the port of embarkation. What the unhappy negroes suffer during the march, and in the encampments where they wait the departure, it is impossible to describe. These encampments become the centres of infection whence spread the plague and the cholera.

The plague broke out at Gondokoro in 1864; it shewed itself at Khartoun on the arrival of the slave-boats. But navigation went on, notwithstanding these dreadful circumstances. Upon the two vessels which brought the plague, the negroes were heaped up like anchovies, the living and the dying lay side by side with the dead.

There is a third region in the valley of the Nile which is also a station for the traffic.

Man-hunting is practised on the frontiers of Abyssinia, where it sometimes takes the character of an hostility between race and religion. The tribes who live on the elevated terraces whence the Blue Nile descends, enclosed in their mountains as in a citadel, have retained some generous ideas with their disfigured christianity.   The Arabs who occupy the deserts at the foot of those mountains keep them at war and in a state of siege, and have done so for ages.

These wars are profitable to the slave-trade; robberies of children are constantly taking place, the details of which are not well known.

CHAPTER IV.

EGYPT.

The slaves who go from Abyssinia are conducted immediately to the coasts of the Red Sea, on their way to the markets of Arabia. Those who leave the Upper Nile also take the same route, after having supplied various places in Egypt. Were the Ottoman Government and that of Cairo seriously desirous of abolishing the slave-trade, nothing could be more easy. In the desert the caravans escape without trouble; and the immensity of the ocean is equally favourable to the vessels of the man-hunters; but in this extensive valley of the Nile, in which the choice of the route is restricted, inasmuch as all transports go by the river, supervision and repression would be easy. Unhappily it is impossible to trust to these two governments.

Recent disclosures teach us what amount of confidence we ought to place in the government of the Ottoman Porte; whilst other facts and witnesses enlighten us with regard to that of Egypt. The witnesses who expose them are Messrs. De Heuglin, Lejean and Baker.

On the southern frontiers of Egypt, to obtain military levies, immense rounds are taken, similar to those of the man-hunters. The negroes are not only made soldiers, but are also used as money to pay the functionaries and the suppliers. M. Lejean gives an account of a recruiting party, formed by a Pacha of Upper Egypt in 1863. This merchant pacha of Gallabat had succeeded in collecting 8,000 men, who were the most grotesque troops in the world. Something more soldier-like was needed, and a vast hunt after negroes commenced on an enormous scale, at Fazokl, on Tagali, at Denka, on the frontiers of Abyssinia, and at the White River.

The Egyptian officers, Mr. Baker also tells us, had the custom of receiving payment in part in slaves, precisely after the system followed on the borders of the Nile by the merchants and their subordinates. This was the case at the time when the English traveller was leaving Khartoun for his expedition to the interior in 1862. M. De Heuglin states similar facts.—"In the Kordofan, the government paid its soldiers and its employés for the most part only in slaves; these employés were consequently unable to satisfy their European creditors, or even the natives, by offering them only this black money. The Europeans must accept of slaves as payment for their goods, or lose their money." Do they consider the immorality of such a custom?

As sickness and contagion spreads around a disem-
barked crew, smitten with yellow-fever or the plague, so
the slave trade becomes of everyday occurrence among
Egyptian functionaries and all those whose interests are
in any way connected with them. Correspondents,
anonymous for us, give to M. Lejean the same details:—
"The barracks are crammed with slaves, they are sold,
they are given to the officers of the government to refill
their waiting appointments."

It is with sincere sorrow that we must arrive at
the conclusion of Mr. Baker, when he tells us that
"Egypt favours slavery," and adds, "I have never
seen an individual employed by that Government, who
would not regard it as an institution absolutely essential
to Egypt. In this way, every ostensible demonstra-
tion made by the Egyptian Government against the
traffic of the blacks, is nothing more than a formality for
the purpose of deceiving the powers of Europe; when
their eyes are shut, and the question is at rest, the traffic
in human flesh recommences in right earnest." M. Lejean
comes to a conclusion equally distressing. "The Egyptian
Government, he informs us, fills the journals of European
correspondents with falsehood, announcing the exemplary
suppression of a commerce which would dishonour the
Sultan; instead of which, the trade was never in so active
a condition."

Are these accusations still true, and do they really affect the present supreme Chief of Egypt? Have these crimes been committed anywhere but in the interior provinces? Without attempting to answer these questions, one result appears certain, which is, that the dreadful crimes which have been perpetrated in the valley of the Nile by the official agents of the government, give us to see that we, as Europeans, cannot trust to Egypt alone to exercise a supervision against the slave-trade. Later still, we shall see that it would be equally unwise to entrust so noble a mission to any Mussulman power. We must not therefore be too sure of good results when we see Mr. Baker starting at the head of a small armed body, commissioned by the Khédive, to bring into his subjection these countries in which the man-hunters exert their ravages. We can believe in the hatred of the English traveller against this traffic; but we can only have a very limited confidence in that government to which the natives are to be subject. It will be scarcely possible for the chief of the expedition himself, in spite of his qualities, to gain our entire reliance.

The expedition of Mr. Baker, which was organised at the end of 1869, with the object of combating the traffic in the valley of the Upper Nile, may give to Egypt vast and rich territories. Up to the latest news (June 1870), it has had to contend with great difficulties. It has, however, already encountered the slave-traders, and what is more, the slave functionaries.

Mr. Baker tells us, that "the Turkish Governor of a settlement of the Lower White Nile (Falhœa), thinking all chance of detection impossible, had made a razzia on this portion of the Shillook country, and was kidnapping cattle and slaves under the pretence of collecting taxes.

"Having received this information from the people, I came suddenly upon him with two steamers, and caught him in the very nefarious act, with 155 slaves, 71 of whom were crowded together in a small vessel. He was accompanied by about 350 soldiers, exclusive of a few irregular cavalry, with which force he was scouring the country. I insisted upon the immediate liberation of the slaves."

Here, surely, is another reason why Europe should not remain indifferent. The question in fact is the fate of numerous races, which civilisation might gain, but which, if they fall under the Mussulman dominion, must be lost for ever.

This great interest of humanity forces us to notice the opinions of Mr. Baker, the chief of the expedition. He possesses all the qualities necessary to achieve the object he has in view, but he is deficient in sympathy for the negro race, and faith in its regeneration. He gives us his theory with regard to the black in his work, in the following terms:—"So long as it is the general opinion that negroes and whites ought to be governed by the same laws, and subjected to the same customs, the negro will be a stumbling-block in every society of which he may form a part. The same law will be applicable to white and black—when the horse and the ass may be harnessed together." The negro here compared to an ass, is compared to a horse two pages further on,—" Like a horse, when at liberty he becomes wild ; but subject him to the harness, and no animal is more tame and useful." Has Mr. Baker gone to take this harness to him? It would be hard to choose between Mr. Baker's harness, and that of the Egyptian.

But we must have more hope for the negro. Let him belong to a degraded race, if you will; it is our duty, nevertheless, to aim at making a man of him. It must be with true grief of mind that any man with the common feeling of humanity looks on the Valley of the Nile. On the one hand, he sees there hordes of adventurers spreading desolation ; on the other hand, the authority which professes to repress crimes—an object of fear, but not of confidence or hope. For encouragement and aid in the attainment of civilisation, the negro has a right to look to European powers. Will he be obliged to look in vain?

CHAPTER V.

THE events which we now witness on the Eastern coasts
of Africa are discouraging. There, the traders obtain the
slaves, which they conduct to the Red Sea or Persian
Gulf, and file off with them, so to speak, before
our colonies and cruisers. Whether this be from crime
or negligence, it is certain that the civilised nations of
Europe have cause to reproach themselves very seriously.
If they have been misinformed, and if the truth has been
hidden from them until now, may they open their eyes
and set themselves to work.

The first country on the Eastern coast of Africa, to the
south of the Red Sea, may be called by the generic name
of " the country of the Somalis and Gallas of the coast."
This region is admirably adapted for the traffic, being in
that part of Africa where the slave-hunters carry on their
recruiting, being also near to Arabia, where the slave-
markets may reckon on the greatest number of purchasers.
There are also there, two places which undertake to pass
the slaves from the African Continent to the Asiatic

shore. These two towns, situated opposite to Aden, are
Tadjoura and Zeila. According to the most accurate information we have, the former exports, every year, a
thousand slaves; the latter sends about four thousand to
the Arabian port Hodeida.

But it is very difficult to find out what passes in the
interior of this country, as the natives will not permit
the entrance of Europeans. Two assassinations have
proved how dangerous this land is. Mr. Lambert, the
French Consular Agent, was murdered there in 1859, and
Baron de Decken in 1865.

The Arabian merchants from the south, run scarcely
any risk until they reach the frontiers of Somali. The
unfortunate British treaties here prevent the cargoes
of slaves from being interfered with by the English
cruisers, as completely as they do in the neighbouring
seas of the Sultan of Zanzibar. When these seas privileged for the traffic have been passed, and their vessels
arrive towards the north, the slavers like to approach
Somali, because they find a refuge there in case of
danger. They conceal themselves behind the reefs which
border the coast, and, if the danger be too pressing,
disembark their cargoes on a shore which is much more
hospitably inclined to them than to foreigners. When the
English are at a distance, after having laid in a fresh
stock of provisions, for the last time, at the town of

Brava, they soon traverse the distance which separates them from Arabia. But, close to the barbarous Somalis, beyond the southern limit of their land, there is a more generous country, where liberty is loved with devotion, and defended with courage. It is a very curious fact, and there is none more interesting, than the foundation of this little native State, which is established for the purpose of resisting the slave-hunters, and which knows how to repulse the enemies of its independence. The history of its foundation, as told by the traveller who has made us acquainted with its existence, is as follows:—

Ten years ago, the inhabitants of the islands of Sion and Patta, with their Chief, Fumo Lotti, surnamed Zimbra, or the Lion, who had been proscribed by the Sultan of Zanzibar, quitted their original home, to the number of 13,000, and emigrated to the continent opposite to their islands, in order to find a larger dominion, where they might receive all those who were outlawed. The part which they have laid out for themselves, and the first law of this rising state, is to proclaim liberty to all those who cross their frontiers, and to provide a refuge for fugitive slaves. In the basin of the little river Ozi, near to Dana, they have built the two strong towns of Vittou and Mogogoni. Ziniba, who is a clever and intelligent chief, in giving liberty to the slaves who take refuge near him, seeks to make energetic men of them, by teaching them at once the love of labour, and respect for the law. In 1867, more than 10,000 of these miserable beings had fled to him; having escaped from the Arabian possessions, or having left the vessels in which they were engaged as sailors; a great number of them had traversed several hundreds of kilomêters to escape from the country of the Somalis. As soon as a fugitive presents himself, the chief of the district obliges him to clear a field, and build a hut for himself; afterwards he enrols him in a company, gives him a musket and ammunition, and each week sends him to mount guard on the coast.

Thus the struggle with the traders is a permanent thing and the efforts of Ziniba appear to be crowned with success. He has gained two tribes of negroes, the Pomokos and Vabouis, who have settled near to him, and give their daughters in marriage to the liberated slaves. In 1867, after having been established only a few years, the little state already numbered 45,000 inhabitants.

CHAPTER VI.

AFTER leaving the free State of Vittou, we arrive at the countries nominally dependent on the Sultan of Zanzibar. Here is one of the very centres of the slave-trade, where it finds special encouragement and facility. The countries in the interior, are peopled by tribes totally incapable of defending themselves; the trade and transport of slaves is authorised by law; the English Government on account of its unfortunate treaties, has up to this time forbidden its cruisers to interfere on these coasts.

This movement of caravans bringing negroes towards the coast is followed by ruin, solitude, blood, and corpses. These routes have a double direction. Some lead to the north-west, as far as the lakes which furnish the first waters to the Nile; the others turn towards the south-west, where a high table-land and some lakes are found, whose waters are carried off by the Zambesi, the long river which waters the Portuguese colonies.

The inhabitants of Ousagara and Ougongo, formerly agriculturalists, have abandoned their fields which the jungle has usurped. Their conical-roofed huts are now hidden among inaccessible rocks. The people fly at the approach of the caravans of slave-traders, who are sure to destroy them, when the opportunity presents.

From the tops of their mountains, they watch the passage of the enemy. These troops of banditti were encountered by Messrs. Speke, Livingstone, and De Decken. They are not like the immense convoys which cross the Sahara, for the route is shorter, and less dangerous.

It is necessary for the caravans which descend from the highlands towards the sea-shore, as well as for those on the borders of the Red Sea, that they should hasten in their march. They must go quickly, as ambuscades lurk behind the rocks, or in the copses, as the native does not spare the Arab when he finds a suitable opportunity for attack. " March on," is the order constantly repeated to the enchained slaves; but when the command is no longer heard, when the cudgel has no longer any effect upon the miserable being worn out by fatigue, he is either killed or abandoned without pity in the solitude. Mr. Baker tells us of a convoy conducted not by Arabs but by Turks: the old women carried off in the razzia did not walk quickly enough. As soon as one was overcome by fatigue, she was knocked down ; a blow from a club on the back of the neck, and all that remained was a body quivering in death.

The Arabs equal the Turks, but their barbarity manifests itself sometimes in other ways. When avarice and danger have rendered them furious towards the miserable beings overcome with fatigue, they hang them. Livingstone, in one day, saw three corpses suspended from the trees; their route is indicated by these frightful landmarks. When they approach the shore, and danger seems far off, the interest of the merchant excites less cruelty. If there are those whom hunger and fatigue have spared a little, they are compelled to carry their weaker companions. There is something horrible and sickening in the sight of such a caravan. The troop is no longer united, but scattered in groups along the road, tottering and resembling skeletons; their faces expressive of nothing but hunger, their eyes dull and sunken, their cheeks only bone. At the end of the journey the boats are there, gloomy, fetid and close, ready for the human merchandise. Here, then, in all its physical deformity, is the slave-trade; it would be still more frightful could our eyes be opened to the moral plagues, the hideous degradation, that slavery produces upon the master as well as the slave.

We can conceive, from the sight of these caravans, the frightful suffering enacted in the interior; but the most valuable testimony is that of Livingstone, whose evidence is worthy of special attention.

This indefatigable pedestrian, whose discoveries have

E

made known to science a great part of Southern Africa, is at the same time one of the most zealous adversaries of the slave-trade, because he knows how impossible it is to regenerate Africa so long as the slave-trade exists. But he does not perhaps speak of it with complete accuracy, inasmuch as he did not seem aware that the slave trade Westward had almost ceased, whilst the East or Mahommedan is as large as ever, and will only cease with Islamism.

Livingstone, by letters written since his last departure, appears now more completely to comprehend the evils of the Eastern slave-trade. But there is perhaps one very dangerous error. He appears at times in some danger of rather extenuating the wrongs committed by the Arabs—and there are men disposed to take advantage of such evidence. Those, who would maintain the treaties signed by the Princes of Zanzibar, will no doubt be delighted to make us believe that this traffic does not deserve so much blame; that we should not be in too great haste to condemn the Eastern slave-trade, when masters like the Arabs are so kind to their slaves. Nothing would be more dangerous than such an inference, nothing so opposed to the convictions of the illustrious traveller. Suppose the Arabs be less severe than other nations, and that the slaves suffer less in Arabia than in any other country, is it worth while to discuss the point when an institution so infamous as slavery is in question?

Let us not yield to the dangerous illusion, that, as the condition of the negroes is said to be always miserable in their own country, it is not made worse because the slave-traders make them slaves. One crime does not justify another. But here the delusion is not possible. The country was visited before the arrival of the man-hunters, and it presented the spectacle of an industrious and peaceful population. After the slave-trade had invaded it, the villages, so noisy only a year before, were depopulated and silent as the grave. This invasion of the slave-trade not only spreads devastation, but inspires the natives with a deep hatred to foreigners, and the work of civilisation is rendered more difficult.

Let us now more particularly direct our attention to the table-land, whose waters run into the Zambesi, and there study this devastation. The Nyassa, which is in the middle of this table-land, is a beautiful lake, whose waters so abound with fish, that the satiated crocodiles almost cease to be dangerous. All round the lake, rise moun-tains covered with forests, cultivated fields, and villages, intersected with a multitude of smiling valleys, with meadows where vast flocks feed, and where numerous brooks flow into the Nyassa, spreading freshness and fertility. In certain places the population is compact, and the villages form an almost continuous chain; the soil is fertile, and the produce varied.

When Livingstone visited these countries for the first time in 1851, he saw the population, men, women, and children, scattered over the plain engaged in agriculture; and as he passed through the villages he heard the sound of mills grinding corn, or workmen weaving cotton.

But after the slave-trade visited these countries, it made a complete transformation. In 1861 and 1863, Livingstone no longer recognised the country which had appeared so beautiful to him. Wild beasts overran the plantations; a death-like silence hung over the villages; the doors no longer opened to proffer hospitality; beneath the roofs broken in by the rain, or burnt by fire, were only corpses to be seen. The Chire had drifted off numbers of these bodies, which became a feast for the crocodiles. Here and there in the middle of the reeds, borne on rafts the sad remains of their dwellings, the miserable beings, when they had satisfied themselves that the passers-by were not slave-hunters, lifted their pale faces, and stretched out their hands for food. When the hunters were nearer, bands of fugitives might be seen gaining the woods; and then would be heard the sound of fire-arms, the cries of the wounded, and the groans of the dying.

The activity of this trade may be proved by a visit to Kota-Kota, the settlement of a large Arabian merchant

named Tuma, who has established himself on the western
shore of the lake.   On this lake, which is only 50 kilometers in extent, two boats with a cabin at the back, are
continually in use for transporting the human merchandise
to the opposite shore.   The following is the manner in
which the hunt is carried on, and the slaves conveyed to
the settlement of the traders.   The Ajouhas, who occupy
the eastern shore of the lake, have themselves become
the allies of the traders, and have received old muskets
which they are learning to use against their brethren
Several other tribes also take a part in the chase.   But
Livingstone signalises particularly the relations between
these slave-hunters and the Portuguese traders.   The
dismayed people in many cases hardly try to resist the
slave-hunters, whose arms frighten them.   The fugitives
leave scattered on the road those who are too weak
to fight, and not active enough to fly ; these are the
unfortunates that the hunters chain in long rows, to
sell to the merchants.   The people know that at Kota-
Kota there are foreigners who possess guns; and it is from
these foreigners, for whose benefit they are pursued, that
they ask protection.   The settlement has become a village;
a little lordship possessing already 1,500 inhabitants.
But all round, there are still 10,000 unfortunates, who
implore the aid of the merchant sovereign, who has only
to wait his opportunity.   This, then, is the manner in

which the slave-hunt is carried on in the neighbourhood
of Lake Nyassa. If Livingstone's book, which furnishes
us with these facts, does not sufficiently expose the part
taken by the Arabs, their villany is established by other
undeniable testimony.

The immense devastation which such a chase must
produce in a country, may be judged by a few simple
calculations. In a period of five years, Quiloa, the principal part of the coast, has exported 97,203 slaves. In
this number are included only those who passed through
the custom house, and paid the tax of two dollars per
head. The contraband trade must be very considerable,
when we consider that this sum of two dollars is very
large, compared with the relative value of the slave.
When one town, the largest it is true, exports annually
nearly 20,000 slaves, will there be any exaggeration in
counting 30,000 heads as the total result of the purchases
in the sultanship of Zanzibar?

One English officer estimates the annual sale on the
east coast of Africa at not less than 45,000 slaves.
Now that we have surveyed all the known scenes of the
Eastern slave-trade, let us make a general recapitulation.
To these 30,000 unfortunate beings contributed to slavery
by the State of Zanzibar, let us add an equal number of
negroes collected in the Valley of the Nile. Then there
are those who cross the Sahara, and come from the country

of the Somalis. If these were equal to each of the two others, it would amount to the frightful number of 90,000 souls carried off every year by the slave-trade. In this devastation, which has never yet been completely investigated it is difficult to ascertain the exact number. To be moderate in our calculations, we may compute it at 75,000, or say 70,000. Is not this frightful result enough to raise the indignation of the civilised world?

But it is necessary to add a last sum, in order to ascertain the real number of the victims of this frightful commerce. It is computed by Livingstone, that for one man carried away, there are at least five left dead: the latter having either fallen in fighting, or miserably perished. In some instances we are told by the same authority, that for one who arrives at his destination, ten are destroyed. If we multiply by five, or by a number midway between five and ten, the total number of victims of this new trade will be somewhere between 350,000 and 550,000. Have the most sanguinary wars been more destructive of human life?

It now remains for us to follow the slaves into the new life which bondage has in store for them. But before arriving at their final destination, many of them are obliged to pass through several intermediate markets, the most remarkable of which is that of Zanzibar.

CHAPTER VII.

ZANZIBAR.

THIS town is the capital of a State which occupies a part of the eastern coast of Africa. It is situated on an island, containing 250,000 inhabitants, and the new route by Suez opens a splendid prospect for its future. It is the residence of a number of Europeans. England and several other nations have consuls there, and it is under their very eyes that the sale of slaves is carried on. It has been said that the Arabs are exceptionally mild masters to their negroes; how far they deserve this reputation may be estimated from a visit to the slave-market of Zanzibar.

The principal revenue of the princes of Zanzibar is drawn from taxes imposed on merchandise, the profitable branch of which is that of mankind. All slavers must exhibit their cargoes to the custom-house officers of His Majesty the Sultan.

The slaves are counted like cattle, and the tax is paid for each head. These unfortunate beings having arrived at the sea-coast—the passage has if possible added to r sufferings. Words cannot describe that which is sometimes drawn out from the vessels in which the merchandise has been packed—bodies, half living, mingled with the dead. Then comes an awful separation; the dead are thrown overboard, the living are taken to the custom-house. But the officer demands two thalers per head, and this is very dear if the slave dies before he has covered his expenses by his labour. The merchant calculates how much breath is still left in each body. Sometimes, those who are so feeble that to all appearances they have only a few days to live, are without any ceremony thrown into the water. This is the first step of the slave in a Mussulman interior. Were they to find every comfort eventually, could that be pleaded as an excuse for this institution, when we remember the horrors of importation, preceded by the horrors of the hunt?

We have already visited the slave-market at Kouka, in the centre of Africa, but that was a market of barbarians, where the negro was exhibited in all his ugliness and repulsive dirt. Here, we find the merchants more intelligent, for they commence by fattening the slaves before putting them up for sale. When the merchandise is ranged in the public square, a servant armed with a stick inspects the blacks, and forces them to hold themselves uprightly: the eye of the purchaser must not see anything with which to find fault, and the merchandise must not be depreciated. The auctioneer who conducts the sale, enumerates the qualities of the men; while he is uttering his discourse, the amateurs examine, measure, and value each one of the miserable creatures; after which the negro is delivered to the highest bidder. The crowd acts as if this sale were a fête; the boatmen, merchants, and the unoccupied, make it their rendezvous; the European alone is regarded askance if he venture in that quarter. Several eye-witnesses have made us acquainted with this part of Zanzibar, the principal evidence being furnished by Baron de Decken, Mr. Devereux, and the Parliamentary papers of the English Government.

But a more hideous spectacle awaits us, if we turn our steps towards the entrance of the palace, which is in the most beautiful quarter of the town. Here are exposed those slaves who have attempted to make their escape. An iron collar attached to a chain holds them by the neck, the other end of the chain being fixed in the ground. A gourd, half-broken, full of flies and other insects, contains the filthy mess which is their food. Sometimes, under the heat of the sun, when their excessive suffering has taken away all their strength, the miserable beings lose all consciousness of existence. Motionless, with haggard eyes, they wait until their master puts an end to their torture. This is the punishment of those guilty of endeavouring to regain their liberty.

The hand of the thief is cut; servants are imprisoned without any reason being assigned; all that is necessary is to give drink-money to the gaoler, and a sum for the support of the prisoner. The murder of a slave is attended with no ill-consequence to the murderer, if he be the owner; if the slave be not his property, he pays the value of an ox. Let them talk after this of the kindness of Mussulman masters.

Thanks to the custom-houses of Zanzibar, we are able to ascertain the number of slaves brought into that island. The English Consul tells us, that during the year ending August, 1869, the number was 12,000. During the following months, the importation was in proportion much greater. We have just seen in what a frightful condition they arrive at the custom-house, and some well-authenticated facts will show us what they suffer in crossing. We read the following in an official despatch, addressed to the English Government, about one of these cargoes: "The custom-house agent stated that a dhow had reached the custom-house after only three days' voyage from Quiloa, where 277 slaves were shipped under the usual customs warrant; no supply of food or water was provided, and cholera breaking out on board, 90 slaves died before the dhow reached Zanzibar."

There is good reason to believe that this circumstance has occured more than once; and Baron de Decken,

speaking of these transports, says, that very often no provision is made against hunger and thirst.

Two observations will reveal the frightful character of
this trade, and the results which happen in consequence.
As has been before remarked, these slave-ships are the
centre of infection from whence the cholera issues. This
observation is so much the more frightful from the fact
that this merciless malady, which ravaged the shores of the
Indian Ocean in 1870, is now re-appearing in Europe.
Among the centres of this epidemic, no one appears yet
to have pointed out the slave-ships.

The routes themselves, which the slavers take, are in-
fested by this epidemic. " The caravan route within three
days' journey of the coast, is a locality generally infected."
A fact, which adds to the importance of this information,
is that in 1864, the over-crowding of slaves introduced
cholera into several of the towns of Egypt and Arabia.
When the cholera appeared in Europe in 1869, and the
cause was sought, it was very clear that it came from the
neighbourhood of the Red Sea, but the real origin was
probably not discovered. May we be wiser this time, and
in protecting ourselves from a dreadful disease, let us
seek to rid humanity of a still more terrible moral evil.

The second observation is equally serious. The Arab
vessels in which the negroes are crowded without provisions, have nothing to fear from English cruisers, seeing

that the trade is perfectly legal. As there is no necessity in this case for concealment, avarice alone must influence the merchants, who think the negro may very well exist for a time without food. Doubtless the price fetched by the slaves in the towns on the coast is so little that it is more profitable to let a part of the cargo die, than to incur the expense of keeping them. No doubt this is a frightful calculation; but the instance quoted by the British agent at Zanzibar, proves that Arab brutality does not shrink from such a frightful reckoning.

CHAPTER VIII.

EXPORTATION AND THE CRUISERS.

FROM the horrors of this authorised slave-trade, we may imagine the suffering on board the contraband slave-ships, which make the long voyage from Zanzibar to Arabia. What must be the sufferings of these wretched creatures when we remember that the eastern coasts of Africa are among the hottest countries in the world? the heat of a burning sun must add unheard-of sufferings to those caused by want of food and space. And these dhows, sailing along the coast in order to find a refuge if need be, must make about 1,500 miles in this manner. The slaves are exposed without shelter to the sun's rays, and to all storms that may arise. Once a day a little water and thick milk is doled out to these poor creatures.

A witness states that generally the vessels lose one half of their cargoes during the voyage. For this reason, in order to understand the extent of the Eastern trade, it is not sufficient to count the number of slaves who arrive at the slave-market. The horrors of the voyage are increased when the Arabs are afraid of receiving a visit from the cruisers. Cost what it may, all proofs of their crime must be made to disappear. Therefore, if the shore be too far distant to land their cargo, they rid themselves of the slaves by killing them and throwing them overboard.

When the cargo has been discharged from a dhow that has been used as a slaver—if we may believe the evidence of an English officer—it retains a nauseous odour sufficient of itself to cause fever, and the utensils retain irremediable infection. It may be understood from the sight of all this misery, that civilised nations ought to unite to prohibit such a trade. But what we cannot comprehend is, that such infamous proceedings should not only be tolerated, but officially recognised by England, which has spent such vast sums to put down the slave-trade. When we see this species of authorisation given by Great Britain herself, the astonishment is redoubled, and one does not know how to reconcile such a contradiction. It is not only an inconsistency, but a crime, for which the English Government is responsible at once to her own people and to the world.

If any nation of Europe or America had claimed such a privilege, the English nation would have been indignant, and yet for a long time treaties signed by British agents with the princes of Zanzibar have formally authorised the slave-trade. From Quiloa to Lamoo, in the interior of the Sultanship, Arab merchants may buy, sell, and transport slaves with impunity. English cruisers armed against the slave-trade may see all, but they must do nothing.

It is easy to see some of the consequences of such an error. English officers are constantly perplexed in their endeavours to distinguish between the legal and the illegal slave-trade. When the princes of Zanzibar have by British treaties the right of purchasing negroes, how can it be proved to other chiefs that this trade is immoral? The conduct of the English not only gives opportunity for crime : it is the solemn sanction of it.

Such conduct can only be explained but by a double error. In the first place, the English nation is in fault for having ignored, until now, what was passing on the east coast, and for having paid so little attention to these treaties. In the next place, it was the fault of the government which connected itself with the Prince of Zanzibar, partly to prepare the way for civilisation, but also in order to combat the influence of France in the Indian Ocean. A political explanation has also been attempted on the ground that it saw to some extent only a domestic institution, and that it would not interfere with a sovereign State. Whatever may be the value of these explanations, it is certain that what passes at Zanzibar with regard to slavery, can no longer be tolerated.

The question is not to discuss the past, but at once to take those measures called for by morality and humanity.

It is now evident that the English Government has been deceived. Since the first negotiations in 1843, the protégés of England have made not the slightest progress in civilisation. This trade which ought to have been destroyed, has developed immensely; the Arabs, spoiled by this traffic, have not turned their activity towards more honest means of living, and they themselves have become the enemies of their protectors. The latter, indeed, when prohibiting on one point that which they authorise on another, are no longer protectors, but capricious masters. Thus their first punishment has been to inspire the people with more hatred than friendship. They have again been punished in another way. It appears that this immoral contagion of the East has also infected them; more than one act of brutal cupidity has made a blot in the work of surveillance which they have undertaken.

This absence of moral principle unfortunately reappeared in the official propositions of certain English agents in 1870 and 1871. Regarding the question from a political and narrow point of view, rather than from a moral stand-point, those counsellors did not recommend the suppression of the traffic, but simply its regulation at present.

They would only have one port for buying and one for selling. The number of slaves for importation should be limited. Vessels legally authorised should bear some distinguishing mark, their sails or sides should be painted a certain colour. Can such a proposal be serious? Can it be suggested to a civilised nation without insulting its sense of right? A crime ought not to be discussed, but condemned. The only worthy solution that England can give, is that made by the House of Commons on June 30th: the trade must be entirely suppressed; it must be nowhere authorised, and the treaties must be annulled.

Provided this project be not forgotten, which it cannot be, England will soon make that reparation to humanity which is its due. We shall see this scandal disappear: that great nation which first declared itself the enemy of slavery, will not continue its avowed protector. A simple determination of the British Government will do more than its cruisers; and now that this decision is made, the traffic will quickly diminish. But in this work of reparation, can the help of the people for whom the slave trade has been carried on, be expected? In the West, in America, slavery has disappeared; not only because of the measures taken against it, but because the public conscience had stigmatised it. Will this moral concurrence be found in the East? Before answering this question, we must consider attentively what the people are for whom the slaves labour.

CHAPTER IX.

In the first place, it may be affirmed as a general rule that all Mussulman countries have retained slavery. It exists not only as a fact, but as a right, under the protection of the laws and the authorities, in Arabia, in Asiatic Turkey, and in European Turkey. Until foreign or exterior influence effects a change, wherever Islamism reigns man will be a thing to be bought and sold; and in all these countries the slave dealers are sure to profit by their merchandise. The slaves are numerous in all the towns of the littoral of the Red Sea, and of the Persian Gulf. Their number decreases in proportion to their approach to the western provinces of the Ottoman Empire; but this diminution owes much to the difficulty of the transport.

The existence of slavery is legalised in European Turkey, though the fact is generally ignored by the West; and it may surprise those who had dreamed of the regeneration of the Ottoman Empire, and of the Mussulman races, to know that this is the case. We had accepted as sincere, certain declarations solemnly made, which seemed to indicate the abolition of slavery. We had believed that the head of Constantinople, enlightened by civilisation, and benefited by our connections, would renounce the keeping of slaves. All this was an error, and it must be made publicly known that slavery has not been abolished in Turkey; that the laws authorise, and the magistrates protect it. It is the English Government which, somewhat in spite of itself, has just made this strange discovery.

Certain of its agents expose with a sincere and noble zeal the existence of slavery ; others, refined in politics without doubt, avoid the subject as dangerous, but at the close of a kind of enquiry which was made in 1869, the British Embassy had to acknowledge this grievous truth. If we accept the conclusions of the jurisconsult, an Englishman, the possession of slaves is not forbidden in the Ottoman Empire; it is not prohibited to buy or to sell them ; the interdict only extends to public sales, and to the fresh importation of the negroes.

This, then, is all that the most civilised Mussulman State has so far conceded to Europe. This incomplete concession is rendered still more futile in distant provinces of the Empire, by the conduct of certain functionaries themselves, who secretly encourage the slave-trade, and profit by it. The contraband of the blacks is an abundant source of profit; this kind of smuggling goes on more particularly on the western coasts of Arabia, and in Egypt. As for that which is practised on the littoral of the Persian Gulf, Turkey no longer bears the responsibility. The populations of these countries engage largely in the traffic, in spite of certain concessions made to the demands of Europe, and they are less inconvenienced than the Turks by the presence of our fleets.

What is the condition of the slaves among the Mussulman people? The laws, traditions and engagements of the Mussulmans explain to us the unnumbered purchases they make. In the administration of the Government, in the works of industry, in agriculture, everywhere, slavery is present. Polygamy introduces the foreign woman into the family, without any prejudice as regards colour. The organisation of a Mussulman household is, indeed, the most unhappy. It permits every home to count many wives. The woman in an Eastern family is not looked upon in any sense as a man's equal; the mother does not reign at the domestic hearth, possessing the respect of all, even in the most noble circles; for in marriage, the young girl is sold by the parents to him who is to become her husband. With this polygamy, with these institutions, so unhappy of their kind, the sale of foreign women is easily carried on. If it is a law of the human race that men and women should in number be much the same, the traffic should furnish wives from the East.

The general phase of character that is met with among Mussulmans of all nations, is a sort of sleepiness and lethargy that detests active labour and paralyses the physical powers. The true believer, it is thought, is made to be master, to command, and it is for the conquered to work in his place. Now that war no longer gives rayas to explore, the slave-trade must furnish labourers, which become current merchandise, given in payment to officers and servants. So long as these manners of the Mussulman world have been disregarded, the Eastern slave-trade, notwithstanding its dreadful character, has rested unknown. It was formerly supposed by some that the slave-hunters were at work for America; and few comprehended for what these negroes were required.

The East was looked upon by us as principally engaged in arts and commerce. Agriculture being little developed, produced scarcely anything; and thus the East condemned itself to an existence of the most miserable character.

Formerly, we thought nothing of oriental slavery, simply because it occupied no conspicuous position: instead of its being consigned to particular parts, and to some special kind of labour, as it was in America, the slave was everywhere. Hence one reason why they reject with contempt the claims of Europe, and retain so obstinately the disgraceful institution of slavery, in which they are unhappily encouraged by their religious belief.

The Koran, which ruins the homesteads by its shameful polygamy, destroys the nation by its exaggerated despotism, and annihilates individual activity by its fatalism. Thus way is made for slavery, which, reacting in its turn, has completed the work of moral destruction which condemns the East to stagnation and death.

CONCLUSION.

THESE mournful consequences of slavery, coupled with the calamities of the slave-trade, should open the eyes of those who may be disposed to apologise for the East, because the slave is materially less ill-treated than he was formerly in America, and in the colonies of other christian powers. The Eastern slave-trade can no longer be tolerated : the necessity of its abolition becomes more urgent than ever. But in this work, it is evident that Europe must to a great extent rely on its own powers. The Mussulmans will never sincerely promote the abolition of slavery and the slave-trade ; and though they should promise fairly, it is to be feared it will only be to deceive. They will never willingly renounce slavery until they renounce the Koran.

This last transformation will most assuredly take place, for we must always hope in humanity, but above all in Providence. But let us leave for the present this difficult question, the regeneration of the East, and the abolition of slavery in the interior of Mussulman countries.

If Europe is earnest in the desire to suppress the

slave-trade in the East, she will prevent the transport of all slaves, and will as a consequence destroy man-
hunting. Almost all these transports come from the
coasts of Africa to those of Asia. The embarkations
which take place at Zanzibar, under pretext of furnishing
the Sultanship, will quickly be suppressed when the
British Government shall have renounced those unfortunate treaties.

When this facility offered to the slave-traders shall
have passed away, there will be redoubled watchfulness on
the line of coast which extends from Zanzibar to Suez.
The Red Sea and the Persian Gulf will be particularly
watched. Europe is well able to watch the Valley of the
Nile, and the interior of Africa, whenever there is the
good will to do it, and sincere and honest men appointed
for the work. But for this inspection and watchfulness,
we must not look either to the Turks or to Egypt.

The great work will become the more easy to effect, as
the Suez Canal brings every day fresh traffic in the
Indian sea. When the man-hunters see their merchandise carried off, when the slave-trade no longer offers
anything but danger, they will of necessity abandon
their expeditions. Nothing will prevent the urgent
demand, at the same time, for reform among the Mussulman powers. Possibly the populations of the East,
forced to return to a more active and laborious life,

having no longer slaves to support them, will regain their energy, and commence, themselves, that moral reformation which is so ardently to be desired.

But for the duty which devolves on civilised peoples, let the European nations prepare without delay. As there is reason to believe that our Governments are about to act, let the people watch and encourage them in the work.

Africa is a land of abundant fertility, but this fertility produces comparatively nothing; the African race is one of the most numerous; but this race is not at present reckoned in the human family. Thus our world is too large by one quarter—a gift which God would have done well to withhold, since we regard it as nought. Do we accept so impious a conclusion? At present there are not only assassinations, but exterminations; there are populations annihilated; there are victims who call aloud for help, whose claims are never heard; there are murderers who have no fear; there are crimes and no punishment; and criminals who expect to receive fortune and riches as a price for their guilt.

What are we to say of intelligence obscured by gross errors of the heart, perverted by degrading passions, the proscription of all generous sentiments, healthful pleasures ignored, lethargy extending over the entirety of a mighty race, the decline of which threatens the annihilation of the people? Shall we remain unmoved by such a spectacle? Are we disinterested in the struggle? Can we, without remorse, remain indifferent?

There have existed two enormous slave-trades: that of the West has just ceased to be; that of the East must, in its turn, disappear. For this event there will be no occasion to expend great wealth, no necessity for great battles, no shedding rivers of blood.

It is for Christian powers, forgetting their differences, putting aside their jealousies, appointing more carefully their agents, and engaging with firmness of purpose in the great work, to bring the force of a united public opinion to bear upon the gigantic evil, when, with the blessing of God, it will disappear from the earth.

————